The Woodlands

By Lucy Marie

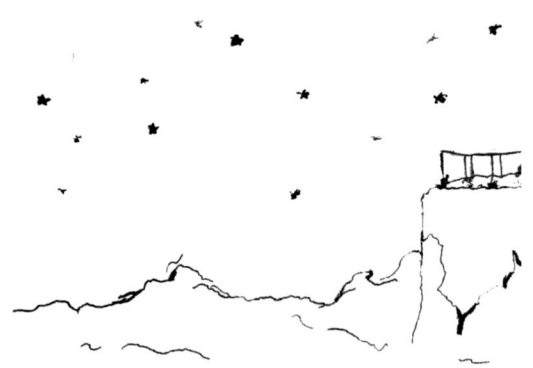

The dogs I met by the river

A friendly one who came close enough to touch,

One that snuck past behind me,

A really really fat one who's belly almost dragged along the floor,

Two in a team but the first threatened to jump into the river,

A large ruby boy who was so so handsome,

One far away that barked loud enough for me to notice,

One in a cosy little red coat whose wet nose gleamed in the sun, their friend, a plodder who trailed behind with fur like sheep wool,

One that I missed until it was too far for me to see,

Two chocolate coated shiny friends who stopped to say hello to a old chunky boy who appeared a little after,

A pack of lonely people who looked like they could use a friend,

A naughty one who barked a lot but said a little hello,

Three in a family one yellow one black one ruby,

Two with stylish purple coats,

A tiny black one who's older friend had a heavy pant,

A little one with a curled tail and as I packed up to leave,

I saw one that wasn't a dog at all but a feline friend for me.

Wicklow

Haunting hills of Ireland repeating themselves as though god was in a trance when he found us. Up down up down up down up down, the water roaring. Pushing itself through cracks in the rocks to plummet down into the stream where it mixes with the mud.

The bitter fudge rolls and turns on itself, making the water no longer clear. Inhale and find that same water in the tip of your nose.

A suggestion of spring has arrived once more.

But the wind is still harsh here. Bitter cold. It twirls around you teasingly. Pulling on the cotton of your clothes, calling it back home. Your eyes weep salty streams from the harshness.

The cold dew on the grass tickles your ankles, trudging through the ground that pulls you down in a threatening manner. Sheep run towards the trees for cover, little lambs following their unnatural fate.

And then thunder begins.

Rumbles and crashes as though you are inside of a drum ring in your ears. A spark happens somewhere in the distance and the first wet droplet hits your cheek.

You run for shelter. Joining the sheep in between the thick of the forest. Your feet begin to bounce softy along the dead fallen pine needles that surround each tree.

The mushrooms peek at you from the ground, their vibrant purple and red colours give warning of their premeditation if threatened. Through the thick you lay your eyes upon a small grey stone hut. Its covered in spongey moss and plants that grow from the cracks in the stonework.

The moss holds many secrets.
Of spider nests and small maggots waiting for the coast to be clear so that they may enter the world in peace. The wood of the door is old, soft and slightly damp to the touch. Nonetheless the harshness of the wind and cold bitter rain threatens to worsen over time.

You are too small to challenge nature.

You give the slab of wood a heavy push falling inside.

And there we are.
Half rotten, scratched from the foxes and blackbirds that have dehumanised us.
The stench is muted from the length we have sat here. We are part of the world in its purest form.
My head on his lap, his hand on my cheek,
undisturbed by the world.
You swear you can see at least half a smile in my bones.
It's almost tempting to join us.
For the first time ever, you feel at ease.

My Only Religion

I walk alone, from four in the morning to ten o'clock at night.

I walk, trudge, breathe and sigh.

Seeing god on a Sunday morning has never been my holy vice.

Instead I see heaven in the garden that I grow.

When the sun sets over the water.
When he mumbles next to me in his sleep.
When the river runs and swirls dramatically chasing the current.

I see a god or simple beauty in each blade of grass.
Every patch of moss. A single honey bee.

I see salvation in every dog, bird, tree, lizard and he.

I witness magic in every black cat, each fallen leaf the haze of incense burning around our home.
We live and so we see.

This is what it felt like

The cheapest champagne clinging desperately to my lips,

Your face, desire, I blink again until I clench a fist.

Can we be friends please?

                                          I think you're really cool

You're some kind of blessing of a person, you're like me and I'm you.

Four steaming bodies in your second-year room,

It's nights like this I'll have flashbacks too.

She's got the voice of an angel,

And a soul that carries blue.

                                        She gave me some tips in a party tattoo.

The Forest Dance

In the still of the night, in the middle of the woods, the wild fae appear when the moon is high. Glowing like an ice cold candle she dances, inviting the others to join.

They tap the head of a toadstool, glistening him with their frost. Taking their stance, the ritual begins.

First a chuckle, and then a whistle as they all begin their movement. They twirl effortlessly tumbling and humming their melodic tune.

An owl watches the mushroom ring come to life with song from the trees above. He turns his head, knowing what mischief they are to bring if caught in the night.

Lights and tiny houses begin to appear, music spilling out of them from little fairy fiddles and bells. They sing in a whisper to anyone else, but up close it is a raucous of sounds.

One young fae sprints out of her toadstool home, joining the others in their movements, it is her first full moon. They gather the almost morning due from the grass that surrounds the clearing drinking the moon water relic.

A frog hops past close by and becomes a prop for the creatures to ride and dance on in their joy. The party drones on, they chant their indecipherable tune of new birth until the sun begins to rise.

The wispy things disappear. Quicker than they came into the moon light. They have no place in the sun.

The owl nods in his place upon the trees, knowing now it is time to sleep.

Our little farm

One day we'll own a little farm,

With chickens' land and trees.

We'll sell eggs at the farmers market and grow all our food for free.

When the days start to get colder, we'll invite our old friends over.

All of them, plus you and me.

I'll bake pies, Jam Roly-Poly.

We'll watch the fire die out slowly, as you play Lucy's lullaby on your uke.

And when its time for them to leave, we'll lay down and love in peace.

Right until the moon is finally sleeping too.

One day we'll own a little farm,

With chickens' land and trees.

And it can be our holy ground, for loving, living free.

Heaven

I know I helped destroy the earth,

One step at a time

But I stopped eating meat in the hopes that she'll be fine

God mother lover daughter son

The ground the grass the water me and you the one

I believe in a life without a home without land that the bourgeois say to

own

There is bravery in the soft,

And sleeping under stars

With owls and green and witches' hats with cold midnight sounds

I'll be a pagan if I must

Leisure indulge in lust

I know it sounds just too ideal, but I'd just like to try it

                      With you,

                              We could lay under the moon

And think about a time when our worries about fossil fuels and stable jobs

and loans and rent and other things existed

But doesn't that take the fun out of existence?

I know I've helped destroy the earth

Reconstruct and she'll be fine

                          The ideological thinking can't just be mine

Don't write love poems

Don't write a poem about how the fresh air feels or how much you love her
Write a three-page essay on how it feels to fuck her,

Hard and fucking fast.
Sweat rolling down onto you like residue on the outside of a glass

Of fucking lemonade.

How's it feel to fuck her on a summer day.

In the daytime,
Do anything for her to keep her from saying 'I'm fine'

How's it feel to have her fuck you back,
How does it feel to become attached; to one another.

Did you tell your friends of how you fucked her?

'Cause one day you'll find out she did you.
And she wondered if you'd find it rude,

That she doesn't want a poem about how you love her.
She wants a three-page essay on how it feels to fuck her.

The Fairy Shop

It's a beautiful day. The sun is beaming at me, I hold my dad's hand. We're camping from what I can remember, or we're on our way home from doing so. We're wandering a quaint little town, with a river that has an old stone bridge crossing over it. It's a classical grey stone British village. With cottages and not a single red brick in sight. We're probably in Yorkshire, somewhere near the dales but I'm too old to remember.

We walk in the sunshine, dropping sticks and other plants into the river, watching them float away with the current. The street that tiny quaint shop was on, the stone path, the right downward turn. The way I pulled on the sleeve of dad's orange and black fleece; asking if we can go inside as soon as I see the crates of seashells on the outside of the building. A door of beads, I'm already in awe, giddy with the thought of what more could lay inside for me to explore.

£5 "holiday pennies" from grandma is fished out of my pocket as in anticipation.

'Do you want to go in?' dad asks, watching my face light up as my eyes wander the building.

'Please' I say back, and he calls for everyone else, they have walked ahead.

Someone waits outside with the dogs as I take the (almost) too steep for my tiny body steps in through the door of beads. The smell of oils burning float around the air from somewhere in the shop. I fall in love, frankincense, my grandmother later would make me a shampoo from her massage oil kit mixed in with lemon-grass.

The floors are dark, waxy and able to hold the scent of old oak wood strong over the already heavy oil fragrance.

Ahead there is a large wooden counter, with compartments that hold a different gem or mineral, rose quarts to obsidian. There are small black velvet bags in a basket along the edge of the counter, I stand on my toes to see the haze of colours stare back at me. Yellows, purples, blue, dark green and pink cloud my vision. 'Five rocks for £3' I place my palms down against the wood to see further over.

I'm too small to see it all at once.

I run my fingers through one of the compartments in awe at how heavy my hand feels once it's filled.

"Little legs, "dad calls out to me "look they have dragons here"

I plod over, looking at what he's pointing at. A fat little dragon, half inside of an egg with a heart shaped gemstone on it. 'July' is written on the front, he picks it up for me, wandering off to look at something else that caught his eye.

On the shelf above the baby dragons are bottles filled with pink, purple, blue and iridescent fine glitter labelled 'fairy dust'.

I pick one up, holding it tightly in my palm, £5 holiday money. All around the shop there are books, "Black cats in practice", "Tarot basics", "Black magic spells and folklore".

I stand there, little as I am, I fall in love. With that little shop, and with things such as magic, folklore, fairy tales and witches. I am sparked with inspiration and the need to know more about this magical world.

Like Apple Pie

Somewhere south near the market, sit hot sweet smiles and cherry wine.

I run my tongue over it lightly, just to make sure that it's really mine.

Apple pie in the night-time, sweet gingerbread little treat tonight.

How come you can still make me fuzzy,

No cuffs just hands come and love me,

honey I swear that I will play nice.

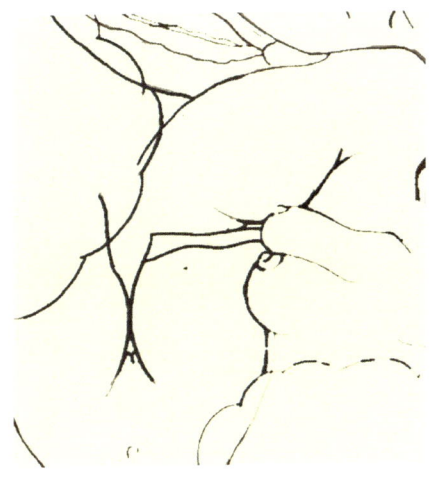

The Rat

A: there it shone/ bright/ and what do we owe the pleasure/ of the day/ good day/ hot day/ Sunday/ she lays out / with anger / he breathed / a pest / pest?/ a pest/ there is/ what?/ who/ WHAT?/ a rat/ and it scurries across the floor boards /

B: and there she lays/ still / silent / what? / who? / WHERE?/

A rat / I watch as it scurries across the floorboards / beneath the floor boards I know

C: a pest? / what is it / A rat? / I lay out / under more than / the Sunday morning / I no longer know / across the floorboards

B: under the floorboards/ across the floor runs a rat / inside the rug / she lays out / the rat / runs over her

A: I scream! / a rat / it runs I scream / why a rat / where? / across the floorboards / my good / my clean / my floorboards / a rat / I scream

C: I scream / hes here / I lay out / a rat / and I / under the floorboards/ Sunday / he comes / shushed under the floorboards

B: She screams / recoiling I say / leave / do not be afraid / grabbing the rat by the neck / she screams

C: I scream / no use / what now? / who / what / WHAT/ a rat / inside the rug

B: who / a rat / her neck / inside of the rug / across the floorboards / under the floor boards / a rat / here because / under the floor boards/ she lays out / what have I done / her neck / a rat / inside of the rug / broken, swollen / she lays out

That Dying Fire

Watch the fire as it cracks and spits at us. Dulled down now
to its embers. The bright majestic being it once was is now an
echo of the past, its touch keeping our cheeks burning now.

We wrap around one another in the sleeping bag of the tent we
have found. A kiss on the temple, I turn back to the heat,
resting my frozen hands closer as though threatening to grab
one of the last burning coals for myself.

There is a sigh of relaxation and we smile. Wishing forever to
stay in this world of you and I beside that dying fire.

Of Funerals & Flowers

Many may not know
  But I am dying,

                              Slowly but surely, I am.
Dying to explore the world with care and intent,

Content with all that I am and will be.

  I am dying to see my children grow and blink and breathe and
              become dying children just like me.

I am dying to bring as many smiles or flowers or happiness in any
kind place that I know how.

But most of all I am dying to do this because I am,
Dying, from the moment I wake and beg to fall back asleep

              I am dying every inch that I explore and each breath that
                          I breathe.

Fog

A gentle fog lay thick between when we are now,

and where we're going.

Summertime ended years ago in my mind, my tan already faded,

I look at him tears in my eyes.

Mascara separated.

We're okay?

Yes. Fantastic even.

But I'm not, I'm breaking down for the third time today.

These memories and creatures come to me in the night.

Their words there to remind me that I can never and will not

ever forget.

That another man took advantage of me.

The greatest advantage one ever could.

The horror of all the clichés clashing and cascading as you sit alone in a room full of people. Breathing is difficult as you feel the rise and fall with such intensity as though someone has a grip of your right lung. A panel sits between your brain and the real world.

Zone out, notice and attempt to zone back in, only to be denied entry back into the real world by your own head. You, your brain attacking itself. You catch yourself singing a song, but the lyrics trail off your tongue the more you try.

The sky looks too big, purple dim light sending you into a dreamlike state. You force a smile, and It's surreal because you know that It's not genuine, or even able to keep you from looking insane. As a second later you're staring blankly at nothing again. And you hope that all the drunken souls don't recognise your face come morning.

I'm the broken cigarette you try to smoke,

falling to the ground.

Putting holes in your suit jacket on its way down.

She who lives in the woods

I've heard of a witch, and she lives in the woods.

She plays with spiders until the sun goes down
and drinks little children's blood.

If you see her in the thick of it, make sure that you run.

As if you take her liking then you might end up her lunch.

Daydream / Nightmare

And to what *do* we owe the pleasure? It is a place for you to be found and find the rest. How pretty your eyes shine in the moonlight, hair glistening and drifting from with the wind. Why are we trapped, and yet graced by your beauty?

You taste like a palmful of water in a draught. Drift. My spirit floats to you as a tumble weed caught in a hurricane. A moth to a flame - a rat, to poison. But you. You have never been my poison. White cotton covers my mouth and nose as I drift off into the deepest slumber.

You are there beside me when I wake. Taking my hand, you guide me through the heavens as an angel would. Delicately you lay me down again in the clouds. You smother me and cover me with heavy cushioned blankets.

Looking down at me you speak. But its muffled, I can't make it out. I twist and take on a new shape. A shape that I have never been before. I feel every emotion all at once. The world goes on. Machine beeping repeatedly in the background. Until the continuous loop goes still.

I owe nothing. Within this wasteland of acid that they propose as a euphoria you trapped me. They did not shine, sugar coated shit. Grey hairs pulled out from the plughole. Suffocated I was in awe of you.

There was no longer any pleasure in drinking when I smothered myself with the indulgence of running out into the rain. Sanity drifts. I'm pulled towards you as a tumble weed caught in a hurricane. A moth to a flame - a rat, to poison. You handed me a rag and I inhaled, although I fade to blackness, I find you in my comatose state.

I stare into the moving picture frame. Clouds and light shining, through them. Gravity rushes over me, all at once, holding me down and binding me to where I reside. I lay down where I am stood, hoping to take the pressure off, but as soon as I am able to breathe again you return.

Standing on my chest. Your sharp pointed heel digs into my rib. They bend and crack under the weight. You sink into me. I feel every kind of pain all at once. The world goes on. Machine beeping repeatedly in the background. Until the continuous loop goes still.

Twin

She is the double and yet the opposite of myself. She holds a mirror up to the water and sees it blocked off, but I see it continue for miles afterwards. One captures moments in words and movement and the other in six by ten squares of printing paper once returned home.

I watched her merge from afar. Through the phone, my heartstrings pulled in a way I ignore rather than recognise. How is it possible for two humans who grew in the same body with the same mind and the same spirit to not be able to understand even a small section of the other. Once twins we are now no more than friends and it hurts like a paper-cut on a chapped lip. And yet I know I should call, but when I do, and they hang up it hurts more than the paper-cut I started with. Same hair same clothes same mannerisms. All I feel we have now is the same parents and the same skin conditions.

Pleading for one to stay for just some company. If that not possible though, how about a cup of tea?

Between the lines

Cascade, s'il vous plait.
Would you still love me at the end of day?

Would you still hold me in your arms like I'm a treasure?
Always, toujours, forever.

Let me fall, let me free. I want to wonder the world with you
if you'll allow me.

I'll show you waterfalls and thick black night skies.
You can paint anything you want between the lines.

I talk nonsense about flowers and wine.
But when I lay with you all I see are French fields, of
countryside.

Capture, s'il vous plait.
Holding you within my arms will be my saving grace.

All Dogs Go To Heaven

We lay there together, in my dad's bedroom before it was
redecorated.
I look into your eyes and I see you staring back at mine.
You let out a gentle sigh, unlike the ones that spilled out of you
when you came closer to the end.
Those trickled out of you like treacle in the rain.
I cuddle close and you reach out your golden hand for me to hold,
your white lashes tickle my face a little as you begin to close
your eyes and rest.
I promised myself the last time I saw you to write you.
And the singular moment that only the two of us existed. The
first moment I felt understood and protected.
And maybe you didn't feel the same. But I know you're safer
now he'll hold you in his grace.

Author's Note

Thank You for reading, I hope you have enjoyed or at the very least been slightly entertained by the content that was in this collection. As you may have noticed if you have read my previous work 'Lavender' this collection has a different feeling surrounding it in general.

Within this collection I wanted to take inspiration from multiple darker, earthier and more whimsical approaches to my writing. I have been inspired totally by Irish folklore as you can see in poems such as *The Forest Dance* and *She Who Lives In The Woods*. As well as places in Ireland such as the Wicklow Mountains (*Wicklow*). I wanted to take an earthy approach to my work experimenting with the textures of nature and the grotesque, inspired by the woodlands of Ireland and Yorkshire. As you may be able to observe from mentions of moss and maggots in *Wicklow*.

In addition to these inspirations and themes though I did (as I always do) want to stay true to the humanity of my previous work, discussing human connections, sex and being in my own way. As seen in *Don't Write Love Poems, Like Apple Pie, Fog* and etc. However, the main influence on my work this time around is to be Samuel Beckett and his work. As you can see in poems such as *The Rat* and *Daydream / Nightmare* I have been trying to experiment with writing things that are vague and nonsensical. Discussing dialogues of death and life's other inhabitable places in a way that connects me to it and may intrigue.

Overall, the creative process of this collection has felt a lot more carefree than previous works. I have not been afraid of experimentation within my work as you can see with the contrast in lengths of a lot of these poems. It has been a very easy-going and therapeutic process this time around, exciting me for the next project to come.

If you enjoyed this collection of poetry you might also be interested in my previous work 'Lavender'. 'Lavender' is my first collection of poems that touch on the feelings of love, loss and everything in between. You can find this collection on my Blurb page as well as through the link in my Instagram if you are more familiar.

Thank You so much once again for reading and supporting my work!

Lucy Marie

Follow me on Instagram @lucymarie_projects

Previous Work